My Daddy Takes An Airplane To Work

LaQuetta "Ellis" Ruston

Illustration by Taylor Ruston

Copyright © 2014 LaQuetta "Ellis" Ruston

All rights reserved.

ISBN: 0615953719
ISBN-13: 978-0615953717

DEDICATION

THIS BOOK IS DEDICATED TO ANY AND ALL CHILDREN WHO HAVE EVER OR WILL EVER HAVE TO GO TO BED WITHOUT SEEING YOUR SOLDIER.

ACKNOWLEDGMENTS

There are so many things in a military family's daily life that is a painful reminder that their loved one is not there with them. This book was written by my children. These are their thoughts, words, actions, and pictures. This was their life for three 1-year or more deployments. This was only a micro-chip of the things we endured as a family. But as a mother to any parent (or other family member) who stayed back and took care of "life as usual," pay close attention to your kids. It gets frustrating for them too. But admire their resiliency. Inspire their maturity and growth through such trying times that most adults can't deal with. I want to acknowledge and thank God for His endless grace and mercy. Many thanks to all military programs, all FRG leaders for your infinite wisdom and guidance in helping our families, and a special thanks to the military families that helped my family make it through the years of deployments. Here in lies Rahman & mine & my children's story.

"Babe, why don't you go ahead and take Taylor to her ballet recital, because there is just no telling how long I'm going to be here waiting," said Daddy.

"I will only leave if you promise to call me as soon as you know your departure time, so that we can come back to see you off," Mommy reluctantly agreed.

"You know Daddy loves you girls very much, right" Daddy asks his daughters as if trying to hold back the tears?

"I love you too" Taylor and Kennedy replied in unison.

"Taylor, take care of Mommy and Kennedy, ok."

"Ok Daddy."

At this point, everyone was being brave. No one was crying, except Mommy.

"Mommy, I'm going to miss Daddy," Taylor cried as Daddy boarded the bus to a secured area, "people get killed in Iraq," she continued hysterically.

"But Daddy won't, Taylor. He will be home before you know it," Mommy tried to reassure her daughter, not even sure herself.

Mommy held on to Taylor real tight. They cried together. Two-year old Kennedy was oblivious to what was taking place around her.

"Babygirl, clean up your face. You have to be pretty for your ballet recital. Daddy will be okay. Let's go home and get you all dolled up," Mommy told Taylor, trying to get her mind cleared.

"Can I wear some lipstick, Mommy," Taylor asked?

"Sure Baby."

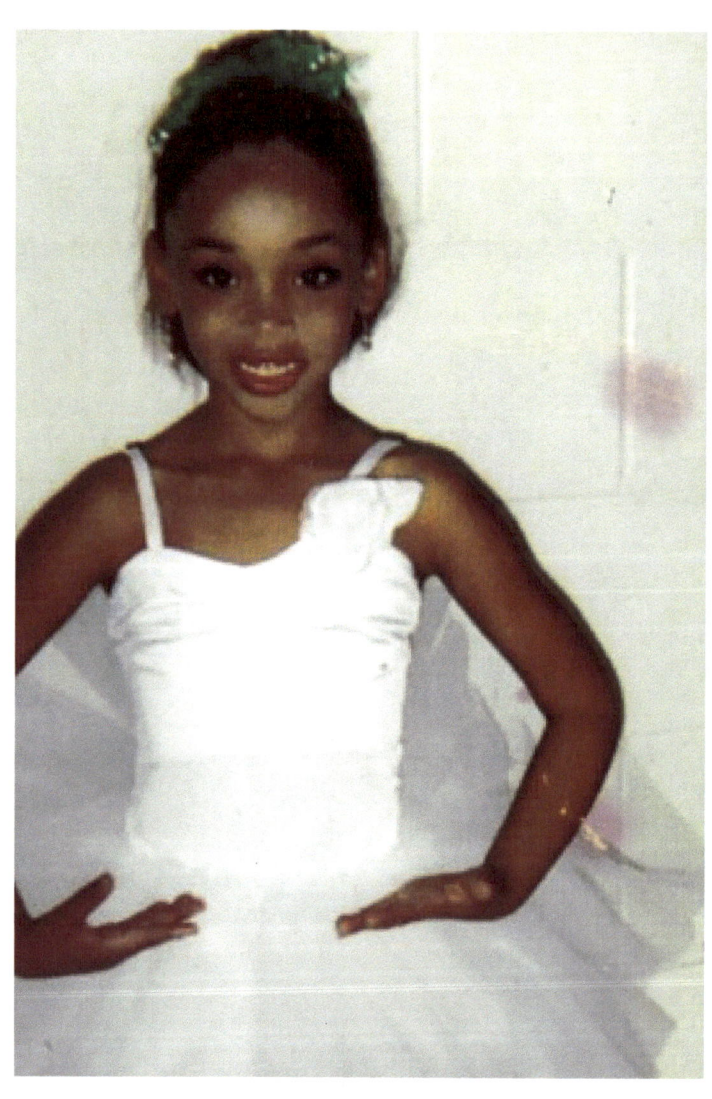

Little did I know, that would be the last time I saw my handsome husband for greater than six months. The next call I received from Rahman was him telling me that his flight was about to leave and that I would not have time to get back to the airport to see him off.

I cried harder and longer than I ever had in my entire life. My heart was so heavy! No, my heart was gone!

The days passed slowly at first. Things they love are now put on hold until Daddy returns.

"Taylor, do you want to watch 'Transformers'," Kennedy asked?

"No, I only want to watch that with Daddy," Taylor proclaimed!

"Yeah, Kennedy, I don't either," agreed Mommy, "Daddy loves that movie."

They bought new movies to watch for the next 15 months.

Memories begin to flood our minds. Before Daddy left for Iraq, Mommy would sometimes pick up Kennedy from daycare, while Daddy picked up Taylor from school. On those days, Daddy and Taylor would race Mommy and Kennedy home.

Now Mommy picks up both girls.

One evening, after Mommy picked up the girls, Kennedy asked, "Is Daddy going to beat us?"

"Beat you," Mommy asked?

"She means in the car, Mommy," Taylor explained.

"Aww, no Kennedy, Daddy's not here to race us. Daddy is gone to work," Mommy explained as tears welled up in her eyes.

"Work?" Kennedy asked, as if she had forgotten.

"Yes, baby, work! Remember Daddy took an airplane to work."

When they arrived at home, Scrappy was waiting at the door as usual. Only this time, he stayed there crying, obviously noticing the missing person.

Mommy just burst into tears. It is so difficult for her to see Scrappy, because he is Daddy's best friend.

Kennedy runs to the closet to hide from Daddy, as she has done countless times before. Only this time, I have to pretend to look for her, because Daddy is not home. I swallow hard to hold back the pain I am feeling inside.

I pull the closet door open and give Kennedy the biggest smile I can muster up. She smiles that big beautiful smile, and is just as thrilled to be discovered by Mommy. But for me, these agonizing moments can't go away fast enough.

The other wives tell me this will pass after about two weeks and life without our Soldier will start to settle into a new rhythm, although, now, it seems hard to imagine.

The next morning when Mommy helped the children get dressed, the heat made a roaring sound before coming on. Kennedy screamed, "Daddy's home!"

"That's not Daddy Babygirl. He won't be home for a long time," Mommy explained realizing that the heater sounded like the garage door coming up.

"That was the heater; not the garage."

"Oh," Kennedy said as if she understood just what her Mommy had explained.

The heartbreaks continue day after day. When will they get used to Daddy being gone, Mommy wonders to herself, everyday?

Daddy calls to talk to the family almost daily. When Mommy updates him on what Taylor and Kennedy have been saying and doing, it saddens him very much.

"I hate this," he would say, "I love you all so much!"

"We love you too," Mommy would reply.

"You just stay safe. We will be here when you get back."

"I had a conversation with the girls last night about your airplane."

"What was it about," Daddy asked me in our rushed telephone conversation?

"Kennedy saw an airplane and yelled out "there's Daddy's plane." I tried to explain to her that you were already in Iraq and not still in an airplane. So then Taylor asked me if the plane would stay in Iraq and wait for you until time for you to come back home. I didn't really want to try and explain all of this to a five and two year old, so I just said yes."

"You did good Mommy," Daddy tried to console his wife. "Let me talk to the girls real quick, because I only have a few minutes left on this calling card."

"Okay, I love you," Mommy said before passing the phone to Kennedy.

"I love you too," Daddy told Mommy.

"Hi Daddy!" Kennedy excitedly yelled.

"Fine," is all Mommy heard on this end of the phone. "I love you too, Daddy." As she passed the phone to her big sister, Taylor, just as excited to be talking to her Daddy, also yelled, "Hi Daddy!"

She turned to look at the phone, as a tear began to stream down her beautiful face. He's gone, Taylor cried.

Mommy explained to her that his calling card ran out of minutes, and that she would be the first to talk to him when he called back. Taylor seemed to be satisfied with that.

Taylor looked at her mother and said, "I feel better talking to Daddy on the phone, but I won't really feel better until he comes home."

"We all will feel better baby." Mommy consoled her oldest daughter.

In every package that was sent to Daddy, Taylor and Kennedy added their own special creations to it. When Kennedy was in trouble, she always cried for Daddy. Taylor cried herself to sleep sometimes, thinking of Daddy. Mommy, trying not to upset the children, cried in the shower or after they had gone to bed. The dog, Scrappy, was a constant reminder of their absent father and husband, because, the dog is Daddy's buddy.

We would get out of the house and do things together and we socialized with other families whose spouse, child, or sibling was also serving overseas, but nothing could mask or take away the pain that we endured together as a family everyday. Sometimes, I would think to myself how much harder on Daddy this all was, than on us, because we at least had each other, he was alone. Day after day, we patiently waited for our Soldier to come home.

"Guess what!" Mommy piqued the girl's interest.

"What?" Kennedy asked, before Taylor could respond.

"We're gonna have a baby," Mommy said.

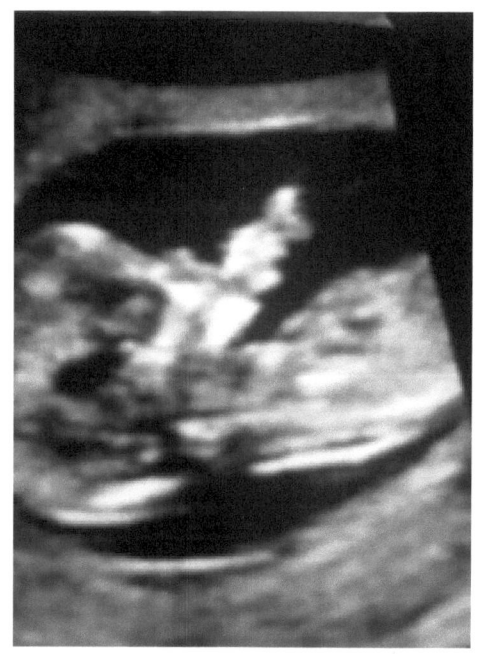

We wanted a boy so badly. I just couldn't bring myself to telling him over the phone that we are having our third girl. So I didn't! I sent him the cutest little stuffed bear, with a recording of the baby's heartbeat. Around it's neck was a beaded necklace, which spelled out our new baby girl's name. This is how I introduced Madison to her daddy.

He wasn't disappointed at all. In fact, he was in love all over again.

Daddy didn't make it home in time for Madison's birth, but he was on the phone the entire time, so I thought! Unbeknownst to me, a stranger at the Dallas, Texas USO, heard the birth of my daughter, while he waited for my Soldier to come to the phone.

But later that evening, he was right by her side.

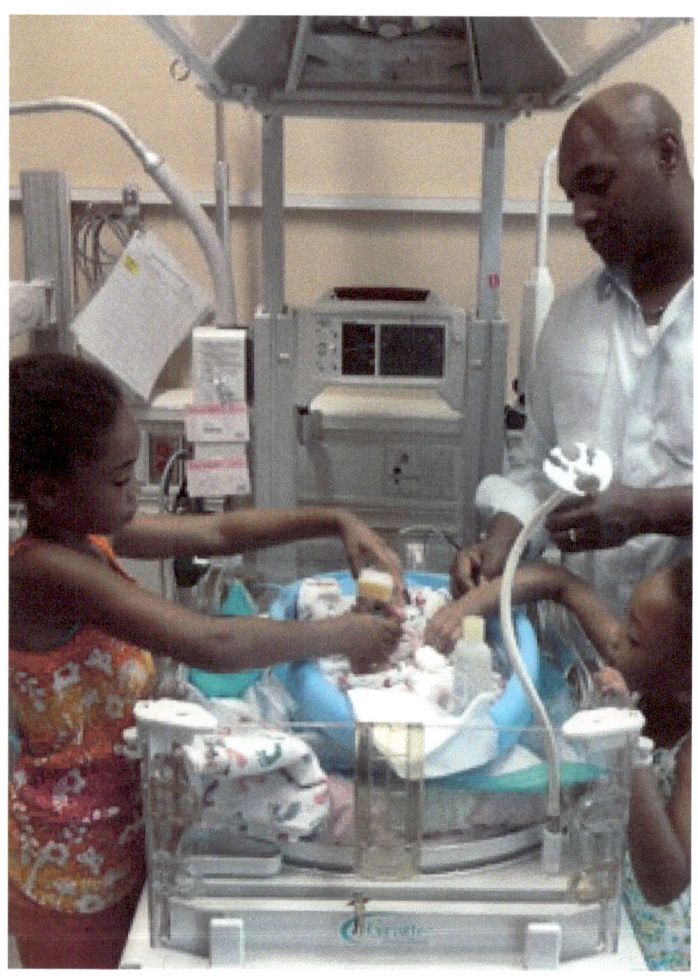

Thirty days later, Daddy was back in Iraq to finish his tour, but upon his redeployment, things were better than ever.

Mommy and Daddy renewed their wedding vows, Daddy took the girls to a Father/Daughter dance, and we finally got the little boy we always wanted. We adopted. With three Iraq deployments behind us, Daddy is home for good!